Neighborhood Safari

Raccoons

by Martha London

FOCUS
READERS®

PIONEER

www.focusreaders.com

Focus Readers is distributed by North Star Editions:
sales@northstareditions.com | 888-417-0195

Produced for Focus Readers by Red Line Editorial.

Photographs ©: Shutterstock Images, cover, 1, 4, 7, 8, 11, 12, 15, 18; iStockphoto, 17, 21 (raccoons); Red Line Editorial, 21 (chart)

Library of Congress Cataloging-in-Publication Data
Names: London, Martha, author.
Title: Raccoons / by Martha London.
Description: Lake Elmo, MN : Focus Readers, [2021] | Series: Neighborhood safari | Includes index. | Audience: Grades 2-3
Identifiers: LCCN 2020002178 (print) | LCCN 2020002179 (ebook) | ISBN 9781644933541 (hardcover) | ISBN 9781644934302 (paperback) | ISBN 9781644935828 (pdf) | ISBN 9781644935064 (ebook)
Subjects: LCSH: Raccoon--Juvenile literature.
Classification: LCC QL737.C26 L66 2021 (print) | LCC QL737.C26 (ebook) | DDC 599.76/32--dc23
LC record available at https://lccn.loc.gov/2020002178
LC ebook record available at https://lccn.loc.gov/2020002179

Printed in the United States of America
Mankato, MN
082020

About the Author

Martha London writes books for young readers. When she's not writing, you can find her hiking in the woods.

Table of Contents

Chapter 1

Climbing Trees

A raccoon climbs out of her **den** in a tree. She goes down the trunk headfirst. Her claws dig into the bark.

Raccoons are **native** to forests in North America. But they can survive in many **habitats**. Today, raccoons are common in towns and cities around the world. They also live in barns and fields.

Fun Fact
Raccoons often live near water. They are good swimmers.

Chapter 2

Rings and Markings

Raccoons can weigh up to 23 pounds (10 kg). They have short legs and round bodies. A raccoon's **snout** is pointed.

Raccoons have sharp claws. Their bodies are covered in thick gray fur. They have black markings around their eyes. Raccoons have long, fluffy tails. Their tails have several dark rings.

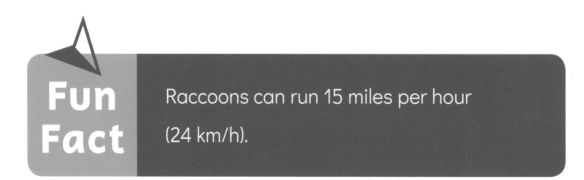

Fun Fact

Raccoons can run 15 miles per hour (24 km/h).

Chapter 3

Finding Food

Raccoons have good night vision. They can find food in the dark. Raccoons also have an excellent sense of touch. They use their paws to find and feel their food.

Raccoons use their front paws like hands. They can grab and hold objects. They can catch small animals. Raccoons can even open trash cans. They take food from inside.

Fun Fact

A raccoon's thick fur keeps the animal warm in cold weather.

Solving Problems

Raccoons are smart. They are good at solving problems. In the wild, raccoons use this **ability** to get food. Scientists have studied this ability. They gave raccoons a problem to solve. Raccoons had to get food out of a closed box. Raccoons could remember how to solve this problem for many years.

Chapter 4

Raising Babies

Raccoons are **mammals**. Female raccoons have several babies at a time. The young raccoons live in a den with their mother.

The babies leave their mother after one year. Most adult raccoons live alone. Raccoons sleep during the day. They are active at night.

Raccoons **forage** for food. They look for fallen nuts and fruits. They may also dig through people's trash.

Life Cycle

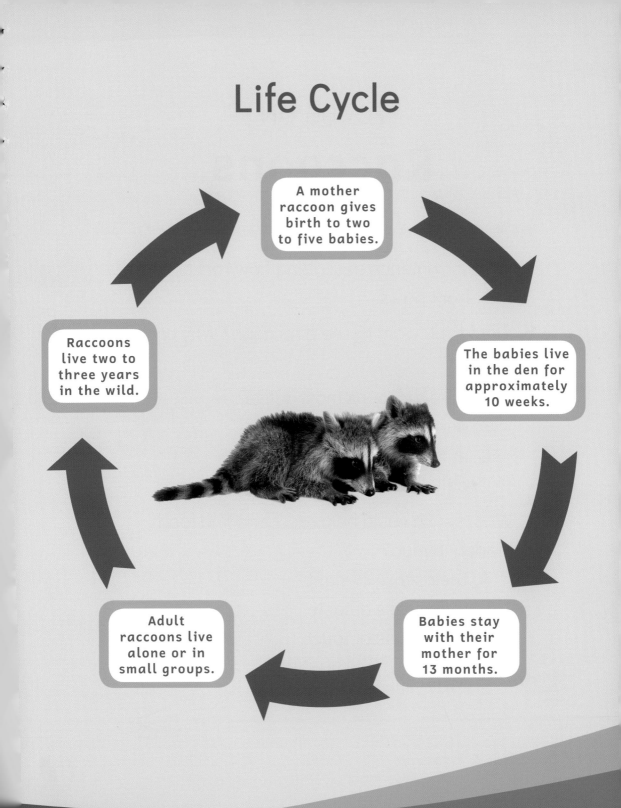

A mother raccoon gives birth to two to five babies.

The babies live in the den for approximately 10 weeks.

Babies stay with their mother for 13 months.

Adult raccoons live alone or in small groups.

Raccoons live two to three years in the wild.

FOCUS ON
Raccoons

Write your answers on a separate piece of paper.

1. Write a sentence describing how raccoons use their front paws.

2. Would you want to see a raccoon? Why or why not?

3. When are raccoons most active?
    A. during the day
    B. at night
    C. only in winter

4. What sense could help raccoons find food hidden in mud?
    A. their sense of sight
    B. their sense of taste
    C. their sense of touch

Answer key on page 24.

Glossary

ability
The skill or power to do something.

den
The home of a wild animal.

forage
To look for food.

habitats
Places where an animal lives.

mammals
Animals that have hair and feed their babies milk.

native
Originally from a certain place.

snout
An animal's nose and mouth.

To Learn More

BOOKS

Albertson, Al. *Raccoons*. Minneapolis: Bellwether Media, 2020.

Duhig, Holly. *Garbage and Trash*. Minneapolis: Lerner Publications, 2020.

NOTE TO EDUCATORS

Visit **www.focusreaders.com** to find lesson plans, activities, links, and other resources related to this title.

Index

Answer Key: 1. Answers will vary; **2.** Answers will vary; **3.** B; **4.** C